COMPUTER PROGRAMMING

in

STANDARD MUMPS

Second Edition

Arthur F. Krieg
David H. Miller
Gregory L. Bressler

The Milton S. Hershey Medical Center at
The Pennsylvania State University
P.O. Box 850
Hershey, PA 17033

Editing and Production:
    Ruth E. Dayhoff
    Dianne C. Barker
    Donald E. Piccone
    Lori J. Doeg

Cover Design:
    Jack Ballestero

Published by:
    The MUMPS Users' Group
    4321 Hartwick Rd., Suite 510
    College Park, MD 20740
    (301) 779-6555

ISBN   0-918118-28-X